KANE

Books by Robert Peters

Poetry

FOURTEEN POEMS
SONGS FOR A SON
THE SOW'S HEAD AND OTHER POEMS
EIGHTEEN POEMS
BYRON EXHUMED
RED MIDNIGHT MOON
CONNECTIONS: In the English Lake District
HOLY COW: Parable Poems
COOL ZEBRAS OF LIGHT
BRONCHIAL TANGLE, HEART SYSTEM
THE GIFT TO BE SIMPLE: A Garland for Ann Lee Founder of the Shakers
THE POET AS ICE-SKATER
GAUGUIN'S CHAIR: Selected Poems
HAWTHORNE
THE DROWNED MAN TO THE FISH
CELEBRITIES: In Memory of Margaret Dumont
THE PICNIC IN THE SNOW: Ludwig II of Bavaria
LUDWIG: The Acting Version
WHAT DILLINGER MEANT TO ME
BREUGHEL'S PIG
HAWKER

Criticism

THE CROWNS OF APOLLO: Swinburne's Principles of Literature and Art
PIONEERS OF MODERN POETRY (with George Hitchcock)
THE GREAT AMERICAN POETRY BAKE-OFF: First and Second Series
THE PETERS BLACK AND BLUE GUIDE TO CURRENT LITERARY
    PERIODICALS
THE SECOND PETERS BLACK AND BLUE GUIDE TO CURRENT
    LITERARY PERIODICALS

Robert Peters

KANE

Greensboro

UNICORN PRESS

Some of these poems have appeared previously in the following periodicals and are
reprinted with the kind permission of their editors:

BLUEFISH, KAYAK, THE MID-AMERICAN REVIEW, POET LORE, THE
POETRY REVIEW (PSA), PULPSMITH, THE TEXAS REVIEW, and YARROW.

In an entirely different version, one hundred copies were produced for collectors at
Kenmore Press in 1978.

Assistance for the publication of this edition was received from
the National Endowment for the Arts, a Federal Agency.

Self-portrait by Elisha Kent Kane. Cover design for Kane, as for Hawker, by Anita
Richardson.

Library of Congress Cataloguing-in-Publication Data:

Peters, Robert, 1924-
    Kane.

1. Kane, Elisha Kent,   —Poetry. 2. Arctic regions—Poetry. I. Title.
PS3566.E756K3   1985   811'.54   85-14148
ISBN 0-87775-168-4,
ISBN 0-87775-169-2, (pbk.)
ISBN 0-87775-167-6, (signed)

Unicorn Press, Inc.
P.O. Box 3307
Greensboro, NC 27402

The author and publisher would like to thank Anita Richardson for typesetting, in
14/14 Deepdene, from the disc by Robert Peters; Inter-Collegiate-Press, for printing,
on Neutral Natural, an acid-free sheet; Alan Brilliant, designer; Teo Savory, in-house
editor; and Sarah Lindsay, editorial assistant.

The number is unfortunately small
of those human beings whom calamity elevates.

Elisha Kent Kane

You shall not be overbold
When you deal with Arctic cold.

Ralph Waldo Emerson

For
GEORGE HITCHCOCK
friend, inspirator, and one long acquainted with kayaks

LIST OF POEMS

*A preface by the author appears before the poems and a brief
biography of the author after the poems.*

Author's Preface

Kane continues the experiments with poetry as history/biography I began with a series of monologues spoken by people real and imagined who hear of Lord Byron's death. *Byron Exhumed* was published as a chapbook in 1969 and was later reworked and reprinted in *The Poet as Ice-Skater* in 1976. At the Cambridge University Library, in 1966, I discovered a book on the exhumation of Byron's remains in the 1930s. The book was written by the vicar of the church where Byron is buried. Byron was apparently so well-preserved for his long journey from Turkey to England that he remains in a perfect state of preservation, and, in fact, has turned to "marble." The result of my meditations was a series of monologues spoken by people who have just heard of the poet's death. In these poems I was seeking an alternative to poems relating my own personal pains and joys.

In 1973, on fellowships to Yaddo and the MacDowell colony, I decided to attempt a full-length book on the life of Ann Lee, the illiterate Englishwoman who founded the Shaker religion in the late eighteenth century. That year and the following year I wrote two manuscripts of over 100 poems each, in her voice. I consciously strove to feel that I was Ann Lee, my sense of her circumscribed always by the few known details of her life. Liveright, Inc., published *The Gift to Be Simple: A Garland for Ann Lee*, in 1975. The second book, *Shaker Light*, continuing Mother Ann's life in America, has so far appeared only in magazines.

In 1976, I chose King Ludwig II of Bavaria for an equally ambitious treatment, knowing that a personage so different from the mystical Shaker woman would occasion intriguing creative problems. Again, I spent several months reading of Ludwig and meditating on him. I also visited his castles in Germany. The result was *The Picnic in the Snow: Ludwig of Bavaria*, published by New Rivers Press in 1982. I have also privately published an acting version of the work, *Mad Ludwig of Bavaria*, and have performed the play at various colleges and universities.

In 1981, I visited Cornwall, where an English friend drove me to Morwenstowe, the remote coastal hamlet where the eccentric vicar, visionary, poet, mermaid, and rescuer of drowned sailors from the raging Cornish sea, Robert Stephen Hawker, had lived. Intrigued by his rare spirit, I wrote a book in his voice. *Hawker*, awarded the Alice Faye di Castagnola Prize by the Poetry Society of America, was published by Unicorn Press in 1984. A reviewer for *Booklist*, writing of *Hawker*, saw a theme unifying all of my work, both the personal and the persona books: "The physicality of life—its messy meatiness and wetness, its inevitable decay and transmutation—fascinates Peters. . . like some ancient vivisectionist, he pokes, prods, and sniffs it for evidence of the soul."

I am grateful for this insight, for I feel that all of my writing is of a piece thematically, and that *Kane* is a fresh elaboration on this view of experience. The numerous persons I have so far adopted (or inhabited) are guises for myself, and embody issues I have examined in the personal books (*Songs for a Son*, *The Sow's Head*, *Cool Zebras of Light*, and *What Dillinger Meant to Me*): the juxtapositions of

Beauty and Decay, of Joy and Pain, of Repression and Exaltation, the intimacies of the human and animal worlds. At the same time, the men and women of my biographies are themselves, and readers may experience their lives without making references to the life of their author.

Elisha Kent Kane, the Arctic explorer, was an immensely popular American hero who is now largely forgotten. His funeral in 1856 was exceeded only by Lincoln's in grandeur, and the area off Greenland where his brig froze permanently into the ice is still known as Kane's Basin. The problems I met with in this work were different from any I had so far experienced. In various ways I had felt I *was* Ann Lee and King Ludwig—Ann's loss of her four infant children (I began writing poetry as the result of my son Richard's death) and Ludwig's bizarre, driven inner life paralleled my own. But Kane seemed remote, a public man almost exclusively. Yet he, too, was driven by immense tensions. He suffered from rheumatic fever, caught in the tropics, which threatened at any moment to kill him. He had to sleep sitting up a a 90-degree angle. Within a year after his return from Greenland, he was dead. Kane was driven by his mortality to crowd his life because he knew it would be brief. He was trained in medicine, had a commission in the U.S. Navy, and regarded himself as a geologist and climatologist. He kept careful records in the Arctic, even when it seemed his expedition was doomed and he would never see home again. His journals, superbly written, were published in 1853 and in 1856. These volumes have been of immense help to me. *Arctic Explorations: The Second Grinnell Expedition in Search of Sir John Franklin* is so detailed and beautifully written I had to resist simply turning chunks of it into a form of verse. He is one of the master travel-writers of the age.

While adhering to the facts of Kane's voyage, I have written my own poems. Jeanette Mirsky's *To the Arctic* (1948) and *Elisha Kent Kane and the Seafaring Frontier* (1954) were helpful. Dr. George Corner's *Doctor Kane of the Arctic Seas* (1972) provided overviews and details. And I have been stimulated by Richard K. Nelson's *Hunters of the Northern Ice* (1969), which contains much about Arctic Eskimo life, ice and snow, and Arctic flora and fauna. My hope is, of course, that my book will appeal to audiences of all sorts. My thanks once again to the Yaddo Foundation for their generous support, to Dan Evans who guided me to Kane's tomb in Philadelphia, to Paul Trachtenberg for his enthusiasm and support, and to these editors for printing many of the poems in their magazines:

George Hitchcock, *kayak*; Anselm Parlatore, *Bluefish*
Phil Jason, *Poet Lore*; Harry Smith, *Pulpsmith*
Paul Ruffin, *The Texas Review*; Robert Early, *The Mid-American Review*
William Packard, *New York Quarterly*; Harry Humes, *Yarrow*
F.D. Reeve, *The Poetry Review* (PSA)

January 30, 1985
Huntington Beach, California

KANE

PART ONE
KISSUK

*water-sky—a reflection of dark
color thrown by open water towards the clouds*

THE NOTEMAKER

I write notes.
My scalp shimmers with cold.
My breaths are flames
cast by a seal-oil wick.
My lungs are gelid.
I'm a slight, short, cardiac man
ridden with fevers,
choking on draughts of ice-air,
ice-fire, as scorched ice. . .
I am also a doctor, a naval officer,
an explorer and passable sketcher.
When the ocean blasts green jasper
or softens into reds (see
its yellowish depths, atrabilious,
meshed) or jerks
towards remote harbors,
I am a gull swallowing words.

I shall commemorate this brig's
motion, under the wings of God,
both in spasm and in sheltered
water. . .An incredible knocking!
The heart, my body's janitor,
stokes rooms with orchids and eels.
My feet tremble in the brig's plunge.

I mean to rise refreshed,
after my smoke-sleep, released—
a key (the self) slipped
into and past slumber.
O, the brains, limbs, skin of my men!
each are parts of me—
part, parcel, and piece!

SEA-FIRE

Pancreatic, visceral
pink, orange, and blue—
tones of mesoderm, as the scalpel
slivers fat: lung-hues, pink
suet slogged all over
the heart and bowels:
the ocean so cold
the foot-webs of gulls freeze
touching it, so alive
it crests and throbs choking,
delirious, with ice-fever.

KANE FASTENS TO AN ICEBERG

Distressed by slob ice,
the ice-tables are demolished by waves.
A bleached watersky:
a signal for open water,
which we can't reach.
We struggle, warp, heave,
plant ice-anchors:
after eight hours we secure the brig.
Fragments of ice dot the water.
First drops of a harmless summer shower.
As the face of the berg crumbles
we cast off.
Crashing , bellowing artillery:
    LOST: 360 FATHOMS OF FINE WHALE LINE,
             OUR JIB-BOOM & SHROUDS,
             A QUARTER-BOAT.
    SAVED: OUR BRIG, OUR LIVES.

BRIG-QUARTERS

Thirteen sled dogs
whiffle and snort, snuggle
against the furbag-encased bodies of twenty men
crammed into a hut space suited for ten:
rimed beards, rimed moss under the eaves.

EATABLES

At very low temperatures
our eatables laughably consolidate:
dried apples are a brecciated mass
of impacted angularities,
a conglomerate of sliced chalcedony.
The best plan is to chop both fruit & barrel,
later thawing the lumps.
Sauerkraut resembles mica
or rather talcose slate.
A crowbar extracts the laminae badly.
Nothing but the saw suits our sugar.
Butter and lard
require a cold chisel and mallet.
Their fracture is conchoidal,
with an haematic
(iron-ore pimpled) surface.
Pork and beef are specimens
of Florentine mosaic,
emulating the lost art
of petrified, visceral monstrosities
treasured under glass
at the medical schools of Milan and Bologna.

7

NIPPINGS

Now begin the nippings.
The first shock slams us
on our port-quarter. The brig
rises by jerks, handsomely.

The next howler
is a veteran floe, tongued and honey-
combed, a single table
over twenty feet thick.
Up this the brig drives
as if some great steam screw-power
propels her over a dry-dock.

I expect to see her
carried bodily up the face
and tumbled.

A mysterious relaxation!
A pulse of ice lowers us
into the rubbish
forcing us out of the pressure-line
towards the shore. We warp
and make fast, are grounded.
The tide falls.
The ice stoves our bulwarks.
It shores us up.

PART TWO
NAPASALIK

*rough ice constituted of ice pieces pushed up
vertically*

THE DOG-TEAM WHIP

Your whip is six yards long,
the handle but sixteen inches.
Flay out sealhide.
Use a masterly sweep.

Sting that husky
with a resounding crack.
Guide the dogs with your lash.

A lash too suddenly drawn back
may tangle dogs and lines,
or fasten cunningly around bits of ice,
and drag you, head over heels
over the gelid snow.

With a stiff elbow
jerk the whip-handle
from the hand and wrist alone.

Thrown forward, the lash extends itself.
A smart crack on ear or forefoot
is unmistakable in its import.

11

MIRAGES: *Hans Christian, Kane's Eskimo guide and unerring procurer of food for Kane and his men. The chubby lad speared birds on the wing.*

Dear Hans,
thirty miles by sleigh.
My eyes are crystals.
A blazing shimmer.

Less blind, you stop my rush.
You whip the dogs into waiting
on a dangerous floe.
"There are no seals," you say.
"No black, swaying, whiskered heads."

The light turns bilious.
Showers of green scream
as the ice-floe graaaks and splits.

A LATE SEASON

Red snow
is late to blow.
A fast floe
for miles below.
Nowhere is an Eskimo.
We have lost our way.

UNFORTUNATE INCIDENT

The sledge we spill
is stacked with *noonghak*,
rifles, bearskin, meat—
our last hour of drifting.
Beneath the driver's seat
frozen meat. I am not cheered.
The route is bleared
with black ice, a fallen sun,
an omen lacking grace.
No booming,
no flowered boughs or daffodils.
The ice divides!
Sledge-runners bleed.
Yellow water overwhelms the huskies.
A chilly grave, this waste.
We're falling through!

HOMAGE TO SWINBURNE

Whether we leap
or saunter, play fisherman or
hunter, we may all die this winter—
and winter begins tomorrow.

Devour your blubber
in silence. Kiss the lips of the cod,
encircle your throat with old whalebone,
keep sane by cursing God.

Trap the swan, that
splendid paddler, and the eider
and the raucous gull. Cache moss
and bark against scurvy. Boil seal-
blood down.

For spring is less
than a season, and winter is never
spare, and summer weeps its glaciers,
and autumn yanks out its hair.

ON FREEZING

For thawing a frozen cheek or chin
a spinning motion of the hand is best—
once you've warmed it on your breast.
For thawing a freezing toe
jump vigorously in the snow.
Depend the ankle, bringing it taut.
Repetitions will dry your socks.

THE *ADVANCE* ICES IN, NEVER TO BE RELEASED

In August we drop anchor in Rensselaer Harbor.
O garden walls are passional / To bachelors and dames.
The cover is set with icy headlands, walled with great bergs
seaward.
    *The hedge is gemmed with diamonds / The air with Cupids
        fills.*
Our little brig's harbored where it will see us through the
winter.
    Goodfellow, Puck and Goblins / Know more than any book.
By September tenth, the ice has cemented the brig stoutly,
frozen in an iceberg sixty paces from the vessel—an immense
molar in this Arctic jaw.
    Down with your doleful problems, / And court the sunny brook.
We are settled for winter, our brig's stores cached on a small
island: Ohlson and Petersen erect a wooden housing o'er the
brig's deck. We have our accustomed morning and evening
prayers, much sober thought and hopefully wise resolve. We
now live home-hours rather than ship-bell time.

PART THREE
KANICHAK

general storage area of an Eskimo house

DOMESTIC SCENE

Tusked walrus heads
stare from banks of snow.
Stacks of jointed meat
planked upon an ice-foot.
Women stretch hides
for sole-leather.
Men cut harpoons for winter.
Dogs lie tethered.
Armed with amphibian ribs
children play ball and bat
among the drifts.

WHITE MAN'S ANIMAL CHANT

My seal, my fox, my bear:
my glazed window swirls with tallow
hacked from your entrails and boiled.
My damp bed smells of your dens.

PLAYING SEAL

You know you are no seal.
But the seal, asleep hitherto,
is uncertain. Disconcert him.

You are a seal.
Stretch out on the ice, arms at your side,
your feet together as flippers.

You are slippery. Lift your head
and gaze around seal-wise.
Drop your head. If you wait

the seal will know you are no seal
and flip into his ice-hole.
A seal sleeps three minutes.

Drop your head again.
The seal will feel good,
secure in seal-brotherhood.

Crawl forward while he dozes.
Stop when he's awake.
Act always as befits a seal.

You may, if expert, kill him.
Grab a flipper, throw him over,
drag him from his hole.

Club or shoot him. If you shoot
shatter his brain or spinal cord.

ON CAPTURING DUCKS

A bolsa is a swift device
for dropping ducks to the ice:
tie ivory weights to braided sinew
and as the ducks come winging past you
let your multiple gadget fly
flipping upwards towards the sky.
With luck the weights will snag a duck
and choke its neck and break its back.

The human voice is fine in fog
for dropping eiders on the bog:
their feathers are so stiff and soaked
their clumsy bodies sailing low
can't veer and swing and bank for danger.
Hide yourself in their line of flight
and shout aloud with all your might.

Slogged with wet, they try to turn
but freezing, frenzied,
drop and churn amidst the snow,
frantic to elude your blow.
You wring their necks with a practiced flip
then quickly grab and whirl your bolsa
as more sodden ducks wing towards you.

21

KANE AND HIS MEN ADD TO THEIR LARDER

She flings the cub forwards,
then wheels.
The cub squeals and cowers.

She leads the furious huskies
to a stony cover.
She is trapped, blind.

She rears, the cub
between her legs.
She snaps her teeth
and whirls her paws.
She faces the ring.
The dogs can't do a thing.

She spins, the cub turns round.
Hans shoots her through the head.
She drops, dead.

The cub clings to her body
then rears up clawing.
We knock the howling little creature out.
His mouth is a bleeding gutterspout.
We strip off his sheath of skin
and carry him in
to our cache of seal and fox—
meat for our final thrust out,
with luck, to the wild sea, and home.

ESKIMO RAGOUT

Kolopsuts smoke
with a burden of seal-flippers.
Each matron's *kotluk* flames.

The Etah use their soup-pots
for boiling stew and urinating.

The nearest Eskimo word for *dirt*
is *Eberk*: it hardly suffices.

DR. KANE WITH HIS ETAH HOSTS

The ammoniacal steam
of fourteen
unwashed, unclothed Eskimo
jammed into an igloo—
temperature ninety degrees,
all twined, covered in native suet,
juicy worms in a fishing basket.

I eat some frozen liver-nuts,
perspire, then undress, like the rest
and cross Mrs. Eider-duck's naked breasts,
pillow my head on Myouk's manly chest,
and, as an honored guest
enjoy a blissful rest.

23

ISSIUTOKS

Issiutoks are evil men:
they conjure spells by ringing bells.
An *Issiutok*, soured, condemned
is harpooned by his friends.
His face, thereafter,
is a flap of skin
trimmed from his forehead
and let fall, over his eyeballs:
he's blind forever.
The people slice and eat his liver.

24

ESKIMO BURIAL

Frost says yes and it says no.

The corpse is seated, reposed,
with its knees drawn close to its nose.

Frost is a sparkle of death.

The corpse is thrust in a seal-skin,
accompanied by the tools of men.

Coruscations of frost enlace
frozen fingers and a frozen face.

The corpse is piled over
with a dome of stones.

25

PART FOUR
NIP

*The condition of a vessel pressed upon
by ice on both sides*

CRIPPLED LIGHT-RAYS, FEVERS

Begin here today: snow needles the tent.
Vexed teeth rip the canvas. Heatwaves drift
from my candle, meant to thaw my fingers
sorting these papers—crippled moth-wings,
gossamer shreds of what we so bravely spend,
crushed between hummocks of ice—my throat
won't clear itself. Crippled rays of light
blear what will be my (our) last testament—
should we freeze and these notes live.
For, as we starve—grim fever shapes crouch,
and the men, sick with diarrhea and scurvy
must either stench themselves,
or use the icy pan we keep beneath the table—
I record how we have pushed further north
than any other men of our race. I record
our thirst for green leaves, citrus,
a female face. I record our hates.
An enormous spill empties my brain.
My heart's tubes clog with ice—
I won't suffer! I say 'wait!'·
I strike whalebone through my heart.

RATS

The rats aboard ship are immune
to sulphur. By such fumigations
we succeed merely in forcing ourselves
to spend hours on deck
in twenty-below-zero weather,
while the rats below are, we hope, expiring.

Our cook, descending to the galley,
fails to return. He passes out
and is retrieved, unconscious.
(First-officer Brooks is himself
nearly overcome.)

None of our efforts avail.
The rats scurry through the night.
They sit on us.
Thank God, so far they do not nibble
our fingers, faces, or toes, although
a rat bit my finger to the bone
last Friday. I was intruding my hand
into a bearskin mitten, one she had chosen
as a homestead for her family.

I have devised traps for the rats.
If we cannot kill all of them
at least we'll reduce their numbers.
This morning, for example,
we catch six near the flour.
We dump them chattering
into a cylinder with chloroform.
I retrieve them, comatose,
and, carefully, with my scalpel
divest them of their pelts,
viscera, and extremities.
The rosy flesh I toss into a pot
add salt and a few dried apples.
Though the result is tasty
I never eat the head, innards,
or the fat behind the eyes.
The scurvied crew declines to sup with me.

CAPE JAMES KENT

A billion tons of greenstone,
limestone, chlorite, slate
rounded and angular, massive
and ground to powder.
Raft after raft of last year's
ice-belt laden with foreign matter.
Symmetrical ice-tables
two hundred feet long,
eighty feet wide, covered
with rocks and boulders
strewn with detritus.
The upper table of the glacier
spreads itself like battercake
under the housewife's ladle.

HYMN IN EXTREMIS

Woolly lambs hop
over the iced hill tops.
Glaciers, despairing, sink
couched on ice-roses, fathoms deep.
One man is dying,
another is snoring.

To lie in God's cupped hand!
To be his celandine, aromatic, musical.
To brush his whiskered lips. . .
One man is snoring,
another is dying.

SKY-WATCH

Reddened
by gaudy midnight tints
the heavens flaunt
bright Capella and Arcturus
those lights of memory.

Where's the Polar Star?
It's not overhead.
Slight degrees
separate our zenith from the Pole's
over which
the Star now glistens.

STARVING DOGS

Alas, our supply of dogs is low,
as is our meat.
They eat a walrus,
and are immediately ravenous.
They whine, yip, and chase their tails.
Some must be shot.
The huskies eat their pups
but won't eat one another—
unless we butcher them.

Today we found a bow-head whale
buried four years ago. We sliced
its tongue—some hundred pounds,
into felt-like pieces.
The dogs eat, and we eat too,
since we've had no meat for a week.

The meat is tough and salty.
We boil it four times.
A quinine bitterness.
We are ill.
Next we boil eight bearpaws
and a deerskin. We boil and eat
shoe-lashings and rawhide thongs
(cooked rawhide resembles pig's feet):
I can't imagine us (or our dogs) more wretched.

35

ICE-PALACE DOORS

Ice-palace doors won't let you in.
Walruses have mistaken the latch-keys
for mackerel. To the south
death-odors broil in pink air.
In this incredible cold
death waddles, sheathed in blubber.

I AM NO PILGRIM

Balconies of disease:
fever-sweat drips
from a shelved portico.
The heart's iron pump
chokes on its own fumes—
it's buried (if my ears are sharp)
at the far end of a glacier.
Flake-worms eat the rusting flutes
of columns.

My near freezing's here,
a nibble of ice-lips.
I will be no stranger to my own death.
I am no stranger to dying.

MAKESHIFT HOSPITAL

Cold water and a low dome of stones.
A habitation, not a home.
Behind it a growth of flowers, starved,
insufficient to cause your heart
to leap or prance. A practicable door,
a stone platform for the ill, a dais
cleansed and filled with wood shavings,
a hoard of cushions, furs. Two blankets
on the walls. A glass pane
(the facing of a daguerreotype) inserted
in the door. A copper dog-vane
with pipes forming a wretched stove.
Tin receptacles for ordure and vomit.
Wipes and bandages (crude sealskin softened).
Paste for wounds, Nothing for headache:
    MR. GOODFELLOW, FELLED BY SCURVY.
    MR. WILSON, SCURVY AND AN UNHEALED LEG
       STUMP.
    GEORGE WHIPPLE, TENDONS SO CONTRACTED
       HE CAN'T EXTEND HIS LEGS.

IN THE BRIG

Like a drunkard or an opium fiend
I inhale the bloody stench of gangrene.
I've removed two feet without the aid
of clamps and scissors.
I can't cleanse my hands!
I've tried rum, alcohol and chloroform.

Healthy men hold down the afflicted men.
Both swallow rum. I slice easily
through the external joints.
You can't push a saw through bone!
Pain's intense as the steel teeth
bite through the marrow.

A severed foot thuds to the floor.
A rush of dogs:
the whips, the whimpering.

The men are in their beds.
Spools of gauze bind their stumps.
No delirium.
I have drenched them with laudanum.

39

DIVERSIONS

Ben Battle was a soldier bold,
And used to war's alarms;
But a cannon-ball took off his legs,
So he laid down his arms.

No amount of cajoling persuades Norton to cease singing out 'Thomas Hood.' Night and day he trumpets the silly words. We begin to fear for his reason, despite his being rather entertaining.

Now, as they bore him off the field
Said he, "Let others shoot,
For here I leave my second leg,
And the Forty-second Foot!"

We get up a fancy-ball. August Sontag, the astronomer, in a dress improvised from brig-curtains, slinks before us as a princess.

The army-surgeons made him limbs;
Said he, "They're only pegs;
But there's as wooden members quite
As represents my legs!"

Every nautical grade writes for our newspaper, *The Ice-Blink*: some of the best pieces come from the forecastle.

Now, Ben he loved a pretty maid,
Her name was Nelly Gray;
So he went to pay her his devours,
When he devoured his pay!

To play at the game of *Fox* is to run a circuit between galley and capstan, all hands following the fox's track. Every four minutes we call a halt, and the "fox" making the longest run takes the prize. William Godfrey sustains the chase for fourteen minutes and wears the prize shirt.

> *But when he called on Nelly Gray,*
> *She made him quite a scoff;*
> *And when she saw his wounded legs,*
> *Began to take them off!*

We pass time as fireside astronomers—but the low temperatures burn our hands, our breaths cloud the sextant-arc and glasses with a fine frost.

> *"Oh, Nelly Gray! Oh, Nelly Gray!*
> *Is this your love so warm?*
> *The love that loves a scarlet coat*
> *Should be more uniform!"*

We play draughts, but realize we must not be trapped by this seemingly eternal day. Despite our insomnia we hold to regular hours for sleeping and waking.

> *Said she, "I loved a soldier once*
> *For he was blithe and brave;*
> *But I will never have a man*
> *With both legs in the grave!*

At half-past seven all hands rise, ablute on deck, open the doors for ventilation, and come below for breakfast: hard tack, pork, stewed apples frozen like molasses-candy, tea and coffee, with a delicate portion of raw potato.

"Before you had those timber toes
  Your love I did allow,
But then, you know, you stand upon
  Another footing now."

After breakfast, the smokers take their pipe till nine: then all hands turn to, idlers to idle and workers to work.

"Why then," said she, "you've lost the feet
  Of legs in war's alarms,
And now you cannot wear your shoes
  Upon your feats of arms!"

London Brown Stout and somebody's Old Brown Sherry freeze in the cabin lockers. The carlines overhead are hung with tubs of chopped ice to make water for our daily drink.

O, false and fickle Nelly Gray!
  I know why you refuse:—
Though I've no feet—some other man
  Is standing in my shoes!

After we had filled ourselves on fresh hare, a gale came up and we sat snug within our igloo reading portions of *David Copperfield* to one another.

Now, when he went from Nelly Gray,
  His heart so heavy got,
And life was such a burthen grown,
  It made him take a knot!

42

In speculative talk, after much argument pro and con, we conclude (with two dissensions) that no matter how severe one's lot there are blessings to be found therein.

> *One end he tied around a beam,*
> *And then removed his pegs,*
> *And, as his legs were off—of course*
> *He soon was off his legs!*

In the midst of one of our reading sessions Dr. Hayes interrupts to report that Mr. Petersen's symptoms grow unpleasant, and that Pierre, our cook, will probably lose part of one of his feet.   Baker may lose both feet. Messrs. Wilson and Brooks are in the same condition, being frozen above the phalangeal joints.

> *And there he hung, till he was dead*
> *As any nail in town, —*
> *For, though distress had cut him up,*
> *It could not cut him down!*

THREE STALWART MEN

Lockjaw grips Baker's throat.
On April eighth he dies.

We bear him over ice and stone,
up an ice-foot, towards Baffin Island, alone.

We deposit him at night,
upon stone pedestals
earlier supporting our theodolite.

We sprinkle snow for dust.
The snow crusts.
We knew one another when we were children.

Schubert, our Frenchman, has erysipelas.
I had earlier removed his foot
with, I thought, great care.
He sings in his bunk
Aux gens atrabilaires.
He dies while I am away
searching for the Northern Sea.

I am strapped to a sledge.
My left foot hardens to the metatarsal joint.
I faint when moved
from tent to sledge, from
sledge to tent. Delirium.

PART FIVE
KISSISAK

ice-piles or floe-bergs

SCURVY

Edema of the feet and ankles.
Serious exudation into
the pleural and large joint cavities.
Purpuric skin-spots
ecchymoses in the pleura,
pericardium, cerebro-spinal
meninges, synovial
membranes, mucous linings.
Hematoma in the gastrocnemius
and gluteus muscles.
Swollen gums, thickened skin-layers.
Fatty changes in liver, spleen,
kidneys and heart.

Bones fracture.
Blood infiltrates bone marrow
and mesenteric glands.
A yellowish skin pallor,
reddened gums, nodules and fungi,
offensive breath, loosened teeth.

An immense thirst.
A craving for sour food and spices.
Convulsions or hemiplegia.
Scanty urine, high-colored.
A tense, shiny skin
painful when pressed or touched.
I drift again, delirious,
to Ecuador, to Mexico,
to the Philippines.
Odorless painflowers
burst from my knuckles.

KANE HALLUCINATES, REMEMBERING HIS DESCENT INTO THE VOLCANO, AT TAAL, THE PHILIPPINES, MARCH, 1844

I festoon my mind with riotous vines.
Red snow blossoms scald a hot brown river.
A million flowers ablaze!
Rainbows of birds swing
through scorched eucalyptus trees,
tangled vines over a steaming waterfall.
The jungle's tongue—see it, there
where the land bellows heat
soaring to the red mountain. . .
my tongue is the jungle's tongue!

My design was to swing on a stout vine
directly down, from the northeast rim.

The feat was to avoid hot steam,
or sudden eruptions of lava.

I would return with hot water
dipped from the murky bowels.

We had not so far determined
the rhythm or depth of the crater.

Nonplussed, I spied a table of hot rock
impeding my straight drop.

I was secured by a stout liana-rope.
I lowered from the nearest slope.

I struck, then bounded,
leaping beyond the ledge, continuing

My descent. I did not linger.
My throat-skin blistered and seared

in its own corpuscular water. Then
towards the bottom of the crater (or

towards the lake, rather) I rode
chilled air. Perhaps

I hallucinated—I don't know.
I lowered the flask

into the boiling water, watched it gurgle
and sink. The rope! The rope!

Signal the men above! I swung out
ape-like, arched up, and over the ledge.

My numb footsoles flamed—flesh
pungent above the sulphur.

They drew me to the lip unconscious.

DEATH FLOWERS

The sky's afire.
Another vile day.
Among these bergs
death's in flower.
Iron brigs and immense ice-
slabs crash onto anchored ice.
Thunder and sulphur!
Sun-dials of death
spin towards and past
and round the Pole.

TO HIS BROTHER WILLIE, DEAD AT AGE ELEVEN

You, dear brother, floating
where the moon sleeps kindly
with all dead children,
return! not as your wasted self,
wasting further as I nursed you
(the medicine bottles leering
on the shelf), but come
wearing superior skin and muscle.

I kiss your lips, brother.
I taste mud among thorns,
mud rancid with skua and gullscreams.

BEAR

A bear laps your throat.
Rancor rolls sweetly
on that stubbled tongue.

IN HIS DELIRIUM, KANE INVENTS AN "AIRE" FOR A COUNTRY DANCE

O where O where is Sir John Franklin?
(Autumn has finally settled in.)
We drape his picture in old bear skin.
Our tears are saltily maudlin.

But I vow to begin again
the search for Sir John Franklin.
To say he's dead is a mortal sin—
he's in Greenland and wears deer skin.
He romps with Eskimos
and eats fresh venison, when the ice is thin.
He stays within during the ice-storm's din.
He likes the smell of unwashed skin.
He lips and nibbles dusky women.
He never wants to return to civilization.
We vow, Sir John, to begin again,
with better brigs, to fetch you in,
John Franklin.

TO MARGARET FOX, HIS FIANCÉE

I could summon you,
could chisel you
from a walrus tusk, a whale bone—
could tongue your ivory-white,
emerald body, fashioned by me,
in peacock feathers, purple boots,
pearl-encrusted shanks, fine lace,
silica flakes.

You see, we are not of the great average.
The scent of your hairs!
I've mingled them with my own.
I am innocent.
You are wise.
Are you surprised?

54

PART SIX
TRACKING

towing along a safe margin of ice

MAYTIME

Those charming migrants the snowbirds,
ultima coelicolum, return.
For the first time since November
barking seal abound. Yes, one of the men
sights a burgomaster gull, a sure sign
of returning open water.
Perhaps at last we shall free the *Advance*
from its ice-prison.

A BODY OF ICE, RESPLENDENT IN LIGHT,
ENCLOSED BETWEEN LOFTY WALLS
OF BLACK BASALT

From its base
a great archway
spews turbulence.
Horseshoes of foam.
Myriads of birds.
Green sloping banks
checkered with lychnis
and Arctic chickweed:
I name this lake for my dead brother.

SPRING: EIGHT VIEWS

1. I pluck a sprig of andromeda.

2. The willows are sappy and puffing,
    their old catkins are dropping.

3. Snowbirds crowd Butler Island.
    Their songs charm our rude housing.

4. We spy draba, lichen, and stellaria.
    The stonecrops are really juicy.

5. Hans bring us seal and ptarmigan.
    The sun shines bravely.

6. A solitary fly buzzed round
    William Godfrey's head this evening.
    He could not tell the species.

7. We are gleaning fresh water.
    The icebergs show streamlets.

8. And yet! Our tide-hole
    freezes every night.
    And the ice-flow
    imprisoning our brig
    is as gelid as ever.

TENNYSON'S MONUMENT

Red sandstone contrasts
with the blank whiteness
of the sheer ice-summit,
at thirteen hundred feet:
a jointed masonry, immense turrets,
numerous, each capped
with a sweet line of greenstone.

One solitary column, seemingly cast
for the Place Vendôme, towers
minaret-fashion some 480 feet,
based on a plinth or pedestal,
itself some 280 feet high.
I am so overcome, I forget my sickness.
Struck with an instant reverence
I name the shaft *Tennyson's Monument*.

INSTRUMENTS

By scouring the artificial horizon I find our latitude at noon 78° 56′ 0″. I soon figure the dead reckoning for the same hour at 78° 56′ 0″. I trace the western shore to a point north of us, where it surfaces purplish bergs and disappears.

We take sextant altitudes of a greenstone's top, and of the debris, with a stepped base of two hundred paces: scree of incredible size and configuration. (A light snow. A four-hour trek back to the tent.)

I am mortified: my thermometer is broken. I'd wrapped it well, encased it in a sleeping bag, certain of its safety.

I manipulate the sextant at Tennyson's Monument. I expose my hands. Pounding and rubbing them brings me off with a single blister.

Our telescope (a 20-diam. *Fraunhofer*) reveals no water in the offing. The floe is old and heavy: I see no possibility of sailing the brig this year. There's heavy, rank ice very hummocky to the westward.

Our bitches are whelping. We shall keep four pups for drawing sledges. Six we ignominiously drown. Two big ones are already a pair of mittens for Dr. Kane. Seven are eaten by their mothers.

PROVIDENCE CLIFFS

The nests are thickest
some fifty yards above the water.
Lumme and Tridactyl gulls screech and caw.

A glacier seven miles at its *debouche*
slopes upward five miles back,
where it passes into a great *mer de glace*.

Ninety degrees in the sun, thirty-eight
in the shade. Cochlearia grows superbly
on the guano-coated surfaces, charming
my scurvy-broken, hunger-stricken men.

Dried kittiwake nests, Poa sods,
heavy moss, and fatty bird skins
fail to burn, so we feast without fires.
We eat a bird each,
and for salad (the best in the world)
raw eggs and cochlearia.

Only two men gaze out with me
on the bleak ice-field ahead.
I pledge them to silence.

NORTHUMBERLAND ISLAND GLACIER

The glacier has two planes:
the upper slides precipitously
about four hundred feet from the summit:
the lower, equally high,
slips at an angle of fifty degrees.
Both communicate
by a platform of slate-ice.
Throughout, the face is unbroken.
The glacier, a vast icicle,
folds and waves, passing round
knobs of rock.

For its lower fall
a dome forms, a great outspread
clam-shell of ice. Worms of ice.
An interior lake exudes over rocks,
suspends in icy stalactites
a hundred feet long.
Melted rubbish foams to the sea.
An incredible din, a booming and rattling—
like the random firing of militia the whole night.

If this route proves rotten
and the ice-slick sheers to the south
among the hummocks,
we may still escape.
This is, alas, my last throw.

PART SEVEN
KYSENENGEK

the south wind

ADVENT OF WINTER

Snowbirds flying south, at night
hover on our rigging.
Poppies recently so fresh
are now quite wilted.

THESE THINGS ARE GRAY

Arctic goose, gun metal,
rat, grayleg, Franciscan,
grayback, whalebone, hooded-crow,
beard, birch, dogfish, hound,
fox, greige, gray gum,
butterflies,
manganese ore, brainmatter,
squirrel, graywacke, grayling,
graywether, graypate—
the insidious tones
shrouding the Arctic for 140
days, commencing in mid-October.
In March, perpetual day returns,
bringing clarity, mist, and ice-blindness.

COVERLET OF SNOW

Snows howl
over a pleached carpet
of grass and heather,
enshrine the flowers
in airless bowers—light
cellular beds covered by drift
beneath which plants sleep.

No eiderdown tucks in more kindly
around an infant's cradle:
a sleeping-dress of winter
about this feeble flower-life.

PESTILENCE

Smallpox decimates the Eskimo.
Cairns of the victims,
abandoned huts, implements
of the chase interlace
along the coast.

Noluk, the graceful hunter,
drives his sledge homeward
carrying meat for his wife.
He sees her through a window.
His infant son, frozen
sucks a frozen teat.
Without crossing the threshold,
Noluk makes his way south.

WILD GERMAN LEGEND

Fresh bear tracks sway
our ravenous dogs astray.
We speed around icebergs.
The Eskimos cling
to their racing sledges:
"Nanook! Nanook!"
We're in a German legend gone wild.

HOMAGE TO THOMAS HARDY

No. No.
Drop the anchor so.
That's the way we do not go.

Still true
The line and scow
Will if we're stalwart see us through.

Still pull
towards the ice-floe's swirl
Where the taut brig gaily spins and whirls.

Pulleys crack
On the ice-jammed pack
The ship thrids with a broken back.

It is so
We can't further go
We'll be frozen in here for a year or so.

EVERY MAN HIS OWN TAILOR: PREPARATIONS FOR THE ESCAPE SOUTH

Three pairs of boots per man.
Three dozen canvas moccasins.
Woolen brig curtains
quilted with eiderdown
for coverlets. Doubled bread-bags
saturated with paste, pitch, and plaster.
Concentrated bean soup, porkfat and tallow
melted down. Ship-bread beaten to powder
with a capstan bar.
We shall rely on our guns for fresh meat.
Three boats, all battered by ice and storm.
Two are cypress whaleboats six feet long,
with seven-foot beams, three feet deep.
A neat housing of light canvas
sustained by stanchions, fastened
to a jackstay. A third boat: little
Red Eric, to be used for firewood.
Not one of these boats is seaworthy.
We shall commence our departure from this brig,
never to return.

HEALTH

I am struck by the fluid brickdust poverty of my nose-blood!
Only four of my sixteen men are capable of any exertion. Iron
is our one great remedy.

PORTRAITS

Morton's ulcerated heel is nearly closed. There is sound bone
beneath. Soon he will be ready for active duty.

Dr. Hayes sadly feels the loss of his foot. He has not seen the
sun for twenty-three weeks. He comes aft, crawls upon
deck, and sniffs the daylight. I fail to comfort him.

Presenting a pistol, I force the blackguard Godfrey back to
the gangway. He refuses to move. I am barely able to walk,
yet must assert discipline. I order Bonsall to guard him and
send for irons. Bonsall's pistol fails at the cap. I jump to the
gun-stand. Cold, the gun explodes in the act of cocking.

From his sickbed Brooks grabs me and says in low bass tones:
"Doctor, you cried when you saw us freezing in those
hummocks. And you didn't quit until we jabbed the stopper
down the whiskey-tin and gave you a tot of it." Poor Brooks.
I ask him not to arouse the others, to deepen their distress by
his display of affection, which display, by the way, affects
me deeply.

DOGS

Tiger the partner of poor Bruiser has fits followed by a seizure. Delirious he runs into the water and drowns—like a sailor with the horrors.

Rhina, our intelligent mutt, is chewed so ferociously by rats about the horny skin of her paws we have to draw her up yelping and vanquished.

Old Grim, patriarch Newfoundlander—his limbs covered with ringbones, his muzzle roofed like the gable of a Dutch garret-window. He plays "lame." Yesterday, moving south, he jerked upon his line, parted it, and was gone. Parties are out with lanterns. If he is snagged, his old teeth can't cut the cord.   We can't locate him.

I have been saving up the dogs who've died of fits. I boil their skins into a bloody soup and twice a day, in chunks, as solid jelly, deal them out to the other dogs. I find now that dog will indeed eat dog!

CHRISTIAN OHLSON, SHIP'S CARPENTER

By violent strength
he prevents our sledge
from sinking through
a tide-pool hole.

When the ice breaks
he passes a capstan-pole
far under the sledge
and bears the load
to safer ice.

Then he slips.
He's under the indigo water!
He rises, extricates himself
on a green floe.

He's ruptured his diaphragm.
His back pains.
We sledge him moaning to the boat.
We muffle him in a buffalo coat.

We stitch his body in his clothes
and bury him in a trench near Pekiv'lik.
We chisel his name on a stone
(he's thirty-six)
and lay it on his breast.
He's covered by boulders.

THE FIGUREHEAD

We dismantle our figurehead,
the wooden fair Augusta,
the blue girl with the pink cheeks,
who lost her breast to an iceberg's touch,
her nose to a nip
off Bedevilled Reach.

We stow her aboard the sledge,
prepare to leave. "At least,"
says the mate, "she's wood,
and that's good."

PASSING FURTHER SOUTH

By nine
we've crossed land-ice.
By midnight
we broach a floe,
cross Glacier Bay, and camp.
Fog.
We've now no sensible position.
Water glimmers in pools,
surrounds every hummock.
We sink to our hips
beneath the watery drifts.
Repeatedly, the sledge sinks.
We've trudged twelve miles.

73

SLEEPY COMFORT

Past all sensations of cold
we are in stupor.
The ice-floe, hitherto poorly ridged
and slippery, is mellow.
We fashion words, bellowing some,
whispering others: a bear
tears Mr. McGary's jumper.
Luckily, he ignores Mr. McGary.
My eyes bleed, a mild sensation
of pleasure—a connection with my
circulatory system.
The bear overturns our tent
but does little damage. So,
floating on the moon, we
re-erect the tent, crowd
into our bags, and sleep for hours.

My beard is a mass of ice
frozen fast to buffalo-skin.
Godfrey cuts me out with his knife.
Oh, the blissful sleepy comfort
of freezing!

CAPE MISERY

The dogs are blown from their harnesses.
We ourselves (six men have gone ahead)
are flung on our faces.

We shoulder the sledge
call the affrighted dogs
and reach the rocks of Eider Island.
The air swirls and darkens.
We must sledge ahead or perish.

The snow overwhelms, roofs,
and quilts us under.
Far outside, a remote thunder.
The wind's a great fly-wheel.
Snow hails upon the surface
of our natural hut.
The canopy collapses.

Twenty hours later, forty
miles of floundering, we reach
the others on the floes.
Thank God, their ice still holds.

KANE IS DUMPED INTO ICY WATER

In cutting the dogs from their traces
I lose my knife. A newly broken team-dog
carries a sledgerunner against a circle of ice.
The sledge is a bridge:
this is my *last chance*.
I throw myself on my back, with my neck
against the rim, and bend my leg,
my soaked moccasined foot against the sledge.
The ice crunches.
One decided push launches me
up on the ice, free.
We save the dogs.
But the sledge, kayak, tent,
guns, snowshoes, and everything besides,
we must leave behind.
All will keep frozen
until we return, to chisel them out.

ESCAPE

Among the Duck Islands south of Cape Shackleton we sight the Devil's Thumb and know that we have come to civilization. The pack-ice lies behind us. Still our progress must be cautious among these fog-bound islands. Carl Petersen is first to hear them—the voices of some Danish men sailing in a shallop. "It's the Fraülein Fleisher! the Upernavik oilboat on its route to Kingatok for a supply of blubber!" We hear of the Crimea, the seige of Sebastopol, but little of America, for no sailors have called of late. The kindly Eskimos fix up a loft-house for our recuperations: we are so claustrophobic (eighty-four days in the open) we are close to suffocation. But the native hymns of welcome soon revive us. Then, a little supply ship on its return to Denmark, offers to take us to the Shetland Islands, where we may gain passage to New York. All we have as Testament of the *Advance* and her fortunes are my two stalwart huskies (I'm glad we weren't forced to eat them) and the whale-boat *Faith* with my tidy store of documents. As I close my account of our woesome explorations I say a prayer to heaven for our successful final deliverance. And I ask that our distresses may ease all future efforts by Arctic Explorers intent on reaching the Arctic sea—for the furtherance of knowledge and the fame of our dear country.

Elisha Kent Kane, M.D., USN

77

Robert Peters lives in southern California where he teaches Victorian literature and writing workshops in an MFA program. He has published some twenty volumes of poetry since 1967, volumes which reflect a considerable range of form and theme. His earliest books (including *Songs for a Son* and *Cool Zebras of Light*) are intensely personal. A generous representation from these books appears in his *Gauguin's Chair: Selected Poems*. A more recent book, *What Dillinger Meant to Me*, returns to the personal mode, and treats his boyhood in northern Wisconsin on a sub-culture poverty-stricken farm. *The Gift to be Simple: A Garland for Ann Lee*, is in another of his modes, the persona book, to which *Hawker* and *Kane* belong. His *The Picnic in the Snow: Ludwig II of Bavaria* is a an ambitious treatment of the life of the mad Bavarian king, employing a variety of closed and open forms. For over two years he has been acting in his own one-man stage version of the work. He has taken the play to various colleges and universities, including Yale, Brown, Queens, Radcliffe, the Universities of California at Irvine and Riverside, Wisconsin, and Beloit College.

Peters is well known as an iconoclastic critic. His two *Great American Poetry Bake-off* volumes have been praised by Robert Bly and other critics as among the most original works of American criticism in recent years. His *Peters Black and Blue Guide to Literary Periodicals* is currently stirring up controversy. He is contributing editor for *The American Book Review* and *Contact II*, and is also editing an ambitious series of Selected American Poets, "Poets Now," for Scarecrow press. Six of these are already published. Peters is a skilled parodist, and has contributed to the *Brand-X Anthologies* of Poetry and Fiction. His *The Poet as Ice-Skater* contains several of his parodies of other poets, living and dead.

His awards include a Guggenheim Fellowship, a grant from the National Endowment for the Arts, and several fellowships to Yaddo, the MacDowell Colony, and the Ossabaw Island Project. *Hawker* received the Alice Faye di Castagnola Prize, and was published, in similar format to *Kane*, by Unicorn Press in 1984.